Memoirs of Scotland

by

Rennie Saville

First published by AuthorHouse 04/26/05

ISBN: 1-4208-3971-3 (sc)

Library of Congress Control Number: 2005902267

Printed in the United States of America
Bloomington, Indiana

This book is printed on acid-free paper.

authorHOUSE

1663 LIBERTY DRIVE
BLOOMINGTON, INDIANA 47403
(800) 839-8640
www.authorhouse.com

The Author:
Rennie Saville
El Sobrante, California
November 2003

Robina Christina Shields Saville

Mother

Introduction

To my family and the privilege of growing up in a country that occupies such a small amount of space in the world and yet it's impact and achievements are felt world wide.

To my Mother who loved me with limitless love and Dody my oldest brother, who gave me a chance to immigrate to the United States. This small book shares a glimpse of the past that enriched my life and gave me the utmost appreciation for the richness of life in America and all its opportunities.

Thanks to all who shared my life and experienced rich moments from both continents.

Rennie

The Family In Scotland

Front Row - Bertie, Cathy, Rennie
Back – Margaret and Dad

Table of Contents

Thatched Cottage

I was born in Scotland on a Sunday, early in the morning, January 29, 1933. I was born with two scalps, some say I should have been a twin, but I can hardly manage with one body now. Life was bleak out there on the low lands and sometimes-bitter cold with an occasionally sunny day. I heard it say that we have six months of winter and six months of bad weather and only the sturdy survived, true for here I stand! Mother was one of those sturdy people and I learned a moralistic way of life with a spiritual attitude. She loved the Lord and made sure we were all believers. Dad was a believer, but he didn't work at it, who is to say?

Mother was always busy baking or boiling something. If it wasn't food cooking it was making clothing, or ironing, or scrubbing, ours or some ones floors. She worked in the dairies where we lived milking, and cleaning the cow barns.

Old Stone Bridge

The old Stone Bridge is about as far back as my memory serves me. I left the house and went down the road to meet Dody and Margaret coming home from school and I arrived at the bridge before them. I was about four years old. I picked up a handful or rocks and saw there was a pool of water under the bridge. A little boy, a bridge, rocks and a pool of water are just the right combination for trying to throw the rocks in the water and make the water splash. I couldn't quite make it and I kept reaching out more and more until I was standing on the very edge and away I went along with the small rocks. Dody and Margaret came to the bridge shortly and looked over and yelled that's Rennie down there and he is not moving! Dody looked over the bridge and immediately slid down the bank to where I was and grabbed me and helped me to stand up, but we had a terrible time getting up the bank to go home. I was all groggy and could hardly walk and finally got home. Mother was in great distress and wringing her towel. She asked me where it hurt and I halfway pointed to the top of my head. She reached over and felt my head and there was a cry of lament heard throughout the neighborhood. My head was bashed in and I need care immediately! Dody got my Dad and he in turn went to see the boss, and he sent his chauffeur and the next thing we knew I was being carried and put into the back seat of this magnificent Rolls Royce. I immediately became sick on the seat on the way to the Hospital. The next thing I remember was waking up to this awful smell; it was chloroform.

When I woke up later my head was covered in bandages and I was in a crib. I couldn't see anyone it would be to upsetting, but they treated me very nice. They gave me a teddy bear and the nurse asked me what I was going to call it, I said, "Mommy." When they gave me soup, I said Mommy makes nice porridge. After a convalescent stay I came home and had to be kept in a darkroom, but I couldn't understand why?

My Mother put me in a upstairs bedroom to recover. The room had an apple tree that grew right next to the window. That apple tree looked so inviting. I didn't like being confined so the next best thing was to climb that apple tree and get down to the ground, and play as before all this happened to me. I lost my hold and down I came with a crash and then I was confined indefinitely.

Then . . . we all came down with Chicken Pox and we were all confined together. At least I wasn't alone any longer! Dody, Margaret, and Rennie double indemnity for him, Bert and Cathie, what a mess, all with the Chicken Pox. We did get to come downstairs but we had to be very quiet. The moral to this story is not to lean over to far, don't take on too heavy a load, and don't throw rocks in pools. Honor thy Mother and Father and don't climb apple trees with bandages on your head.

Things were all starting to come into place and I was starting to get the grasp of things. The old Stone Bridge spanned a small river leading to the River Nith, a tributary, where the fishing was very good. I had an intense interest and my Dad as an expert with a fishing rod and fly tying, to this day it holds a special fascination for me.

The Potato Patch

In the fall we got two weeks off from school to pick potatoes. That was a nightmare for me. I was to skinny to drag the heavy basket along and Margaret (my sister who was two (2) years older than me) was always after me to keep up and bring the basket that kept getting full. The potato spreader was right there with the driver always yelling to hurry up, the big boss would come by and he would yell to hurry. He would threaten no pay for us two if we didn't hurry up and pick our potatoes but at the end of the day we would hear, "Rennie, Margaret", and we would hurry to get our envelopes with our pay. Then he would say you better hurry up or tomorrow no pay. But we always got our pay. Sometimes I would be so hungry I could hardly walk let alone work picking potatoes. Mother was always encouraging me to do my best and told me everyone has to do their share of work. I tried to, but it was very hard to do.

I was the black sheep of the family, the only one with black hair, my sisters and brothers had blond or red hair! My family consisted of George (Dody), Margaret, Bert, Catherine (Cathy), and me. We idolized Dody; he was the peacemaker and chief adviser for us kids. Bert and I were like two otters, always wrestling and never still a minute.

My favorite thing to do was roaming down the glen or climbing Criffel Mountain, rabbit hunting, or cutting wood with a buck saw making sure there was plenty cut or there was a tongue lashing in order.

 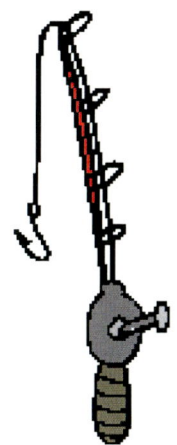

Fishing

When the black clouds started to gather it was time to dig worms and get the fishing poles ready! The big brown trout were awake and hungry and in the brook that ran past the house. They were a prize to behold and were about six to eight inches long and could give you a fight you wouldn't forget soon. When the water started to get brown (runoff from the mountains) we knew that the fishing was over and to head for home, but not without the prize 4, 5, or 6 of the best trout you laid your eyes on and made the heart glad. Bert and I would have to go to Kelton Bank for flounders on a Friday after school. We would take our burlap sack and go to the fishmonger and he would let us pick out the ones we liked. Now it was a good long walk down there to where we got the flounders and on the way back, there were these boys always waiting and try to take our fish. To say the least the fight was on and the noses bled or eyes got bruised but we never lost the fish and they said we stank! They left boasting obscenities at us.

The Out-house

We had a good size garden, down at the end of the garden path there was an out- house made of red bricks. Quite adorable for an out-house but no windows. I got the bright idea of cutting a window in the south wall. I dug around for tools and found a chisel and a hammer and proceeded to cut out a window! Even at the age of six or seven my carpenter career was budding. I drew a line in a square the size I thought a window should be. I started with great enthusiasm after working about two hours—without warning—my feet sort of left the ground and I was floating through the air. My Dad had come out to use the out-house and saw me working there and snuck up on me and carried me into the house. Off came his big belt and he gave me a good belting, which brought me back to earth and an explanation of, "ask first."

The Doll

Down the hall and to the left was Margaret and Cathie's room and in that room they had this doll, what a beautiful doll with a fancy dress, fair lady shoes and the most beautiful eyes that rolled back and went to sleep when you laid the doll down. It made a crying noise that started something in me to find out what caused these things to happen. Brother Bert and I waited for the right time and before you knew it we had that doll and took it apart piece by piece and in no orderly fashion. Out popped its eyes and we finally got the strings that worked the eyes, out they came when the doll fell to the floor it made a louder noise than usual. Margaret and Cathie heard the noise and came into the room screaming incessantly with anguish and looked at us with daggers of hate. Mother saw what had happened and joined in the fierce attack and called for Dad who came and promptly joined in the assault. I knew a flogging was in order, but only a tongue-lashing and a light belting ensued, always be sure to look down at the floor, a sure sign of defeat.

The Motorcycle

My cousin Peter Magchie* came to visit, he rode dispatch in World War II, he invited Dad to learn to ride his motorcycle. My father exuded confidence as he mounted the motorcycle; he took a back road that sort of went downhill with Hawthorn trees on both sides. He gained confidence and went a little faster, when he was struck with fear and grabbed for the brake. Due to his inexperience he rolled open the throttle and lost control. He hung on to the motorcycle as it left the road and the Hawthorn bushes were waiting for him. He was pulled through a hedge backwards, "is an understatement." He was thoroughly lodged in the crotch of a Hawthorn bush and had to be pulled out. He was in a daze, stupefied, or stunned state, he was a stranger to us and called us his poor children with a display of affection and compassion, we knew he wasn't right. He sat there with glassy eyes but quite soon he came to and told us to get away from him, then we knew he was back to normal

––––––––––––––––.
*Peter Magchie was severely wounded in WWII, a very handsome man, he survived the war; however, his face, fingers and legs were blown off. He would have lost his life but due to the speed he was traveling saved his life.

Elegant Feast

At the end of the school year all the children were invited to a party at an "Estate." This was the biggest house I had ever seen. It was beautiful with flowers everywhere, grand grounds, and gardens. We were invited to the inner garden and seated at a magnificent banquet table. I was seated on a high back chair like a throne. It made me feel superior. After we were seated and the noise settled down, they started to bring in trays of food, everything was delicious, then came another tray, and another, there was no end. I kept taking food, eating, there was no more room on my plate, I put it on my lap then I reached around and started piling the food up, taking more than one helping and putting it on the chair behind me. I kept piling the food up due to my greed. I could see lines of ladies all bedecked with ribbons, lace, and flowers carrying trays of more food more than I had ever seen in my life. Sandwiches cut like diamonds, circles, etc. Every design you could think of, I ate and ate. I was stuffed, then came the cakes and more cakes the ladies came by with every kind of desert. Not one tray went by that I didn't take a cake or something off it and put it behind me. The space behind me was diminishing fast. I ate until my eyes started to bulge and suddenly it was over--time to go home! We had to stand up and get in line for the bus, what was I to do, so I stood up and all the other children had done the same thing. We left and had to leave the huge mountains of food on the chairs with much embarassment. The party was a huge success!

Dying for a Cigarette

I remember it was a Saturday and the weather was clear, we had to go down to the forest to cut some dead trees for firewood and kindling, it was hard work. Just before we started my dad said, "go down to the store and get me some cigarettes, I am dying for a cigarette!" I was stunned, dying? How could he be dying? We were cutting wood! He gave me some money and off I sped to the store as fast as I could go sweating and breathless, I reached the store and asked for 5 Wild Woodbine cigarettes. I paid for them and raced back to Dad. I was thinking he would be lying there dying, how could I face that? My dad is dying! Suddenly I was there with the cigarettes. I ran over to him and gave him the (five) Wild Woodbines and he said to me, "put them over there on the stump!" All the blood drained out of me, I thought I was going to faint, when I recovered, hate overwhelmed me and a great separation came between us. He was just a person not a Dad to adore, love and honor. I grew up that day.

Gathering Gull Eggs

In late spring we to went down to the moors to pick gull eggs they are a delicious plate for hungry people. We didn't find many that day and were about to pack it in when someone said, "look over there." No one could make it out except the old farmer, he said, "it was a swarm of bees." We went closer and sure enough it was a bee swarm. They hung on the lowest branch on a six-foot tree; it was the only tree of any kind around as far as you could see. Someone suggested we take them home. We had nothing to carry them in "yes we do", said the old farmer, Jim take your shirt off and take your hat off Tom. Put your hat down inside the shirt and sweep the swarm up on both sides and snap off the branch and we can carry it home that way. We took a vote on who would carry that branch all the way home. I was the one voted in as to the one who would carry it. The smallest, and weakest, well I lost the vote, Jim grabbed one side of the shirt and I the other and up over the bees the shirt went and up to the branch. We diligently broke the branch off, I was tempted to drop it and run like hell but everyone was encouraging me you can do it, but on one occasion I almost fell and I thought my arms were going to break off. The noise of the bees in the shirt kept me in a straight line for home. I made it with every ounce I could muster. The old farmer got out an apple box and a door. He notched the apple box and put it on the door that he had sloped up on the stone wall, then he said, if you don't like bees get away. I liked bees enough to carry them from the moors. The old farmer took the bees and dumped them out on the door and with his hands guided them into the apple box. One by one and two by two they went into their new home. The farmer exclaimed, "if the queen is in the swarm they will stay." Well I guess the queen reigned supreme, they stayed!

The Wheel

We went to visit Jock, ("Bill" Mrs. Cousins), and Graham, Jock's son. Jock was a truck driver and was on the road a lot hauling sheep and bulls to the slaughterhouse. They had a garage near by and were changing tires. It was sort of on the street and someone leaned the truck wheel against the door that closes the place up. That sort of set things in motion, this big heavy wheel started to roll down the hill and before anyone could react it was gaining speed and was out of reach. Everyone was screaming and yelling and the wheel was heading for the downtown without hitting anyone, but it did take a glancing blow on the stone wall that aimed it right down the middle of the street, it disappeared around the bend as the street curved to the right. That aimed the wheel straight for the grocery store, We heard this God awful crash as the wheel went through the plate glass window and destroyed the inside of the grocery store. No one was hurt just amazed at how this invisible hand guided the wheel without causing loss or injury to anyone!

Visits to Grandpa

Grandpa lived in a single room; he had a fireplace for heat – that is where my Grandpa lived. He smoked a pipe and everything smelled so sweet, the smoke from his pipe and the fireplace made it all the more delectable. He had the most beautiful feather bed, when you got into the bed you started sinking and before you stopped sinking you were asleep before you hit the bottom. We would go down and stay with him; he would scrape out his pipe into his hand and mix in the new tobacco. His hands were so tough he couldn't feel the burning tobacco. When he was a young man he was kicked by a horse, it broke his lower jaw and deformed it along with his lower lip. It also affected his hearing and you had to speak up close right into his ear. He called everyone "Wee Sonny" or "Sonny" depending on your size, he was a humble man and everyone liked him. Every Saturday night he would go into town and have a few beers and visit his old pals and wear his beautiful gold watch in his waistcoat, suit, and shined shoes. When he hopped the last bus to come home, as he would get near his stop and tell the driver to wait, he had to pee. He would get off the bus and go around to the front of the bus so he could see, then he would wave the driver on and away he would go down the road swaying slightly but in full control.

Grandpa got sick and it looked as if he would not recover, he decided to stay with Aunt Gaggy and Aunt Jean. They were sure he was going to die so they ordered a coffin. A few days later up he popped, Grandpa went back to work driving fence posts with a sixteen pound hammer and never looked back. This happened again and again, they ordered a coffin but he survived and lived a good many more productive years. When he finally did pass away he was missed by all especially by me, my Grandpa a passing love, the teacher, a kind and gentle man. I don't know if he was a believer or not. Someday I hope we'll meet again.

Picking Black Currents

We were sitting around the table eating dinner on a Saturday night when Dad announced that we had to pick the black currents tomorrow, and my heart sank. Do you know what kind of job that is? Millions and million of those tiny little things, I hated that job worse than anything. It was an all day job and your hands got all stained black. We got our buckets ready for next morning so we could get it over with. There were six l-o-n-g rows and they were totally loaded. I spent a restless night thinking about those berries to pick the next day. Sunday morning came, we got up and ate our porridge and went out to the berry patch. To our amazement there was not one berry on the bushes. Someone had come in during the night and picked every last one and took our buckets also. Dad was very upset, we kept out of the way in case he went into a rage! Bert and I were sad about it but happy we didn't have to pick those berries. Dad was a good fighter and he was ready to knock someone's head off. He had suspicions but no proof. It could have been a band of Gypsies, so many berries gone. . .

<<<>>>

Fishing, Ducks and Flounder

You could follow the brook up into the hills as it narrowed, and become smaller and smaller it led you further up the hills. Then it would turn into the right size, width, and depth for you to start guddeling. Guddeling is when you put your hands under the water and feel around the bottom of the rocks to find an opening for the trout to hide under this is "the lair of the trout." You could block the opening, if you were fast enough, and try to gill him, "get your fingers into the gills." Then the trout was yours.

We would cut up some potatoes and half cook them and put them on a string across the bog, leaving it overnight. In the morning we had to be early to outsmart Mr. Fox. We checked our lines, some of the ducks were hanging there, some had flown away, and some were dying. We had our ducks without a shot fired. What a bounty, nice big fat ducks we didn't mind cleaning the ducks, umm-roast duck, roasted potatoes and Yorkshire Pudding, the best in the world.

The tide, rises and ebbs twice a day on the River Nith when it was low tide or a minus tide Dad would take two posts and dig them into each side of the river and make them very secure. He would tie a heavy gauge wire to each post and hang lines down about two feet apart all the way across the river. He would bait each hook, then wait for the tide to come in and wait again for the tide to go out. There would be a delicious flounder or cod hanging on the line! He would go to the side of the river and swing the line to one side. We would take the fish off and put them in a wet burlap sack and head for home with the prize catch. When Dad was fishing we picked mushrooms. They grew on the banks of the river, in an occasional sunny spot. Mushrooms fried in butter are very good. I ate many a pan full of mushrooms. We were taught to select the edible mushrooms from the poisonous. We only rarely came across a poisonous mushroom. A good mushroom is creamy white on top and pink on the underside. We would pick them and check the underside if it was dark we threw it away.

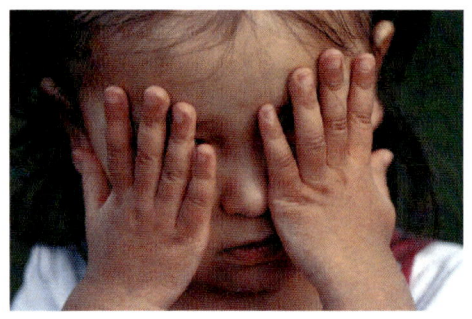

Aunt Jennie

I had an Aunt Jennie but we won't talk about, "her", she had to be the most cruel woman I ever met in my whole life. I detested her, which I had no right to do. Jake McLaughlin her husband, through circumstance got drunk for the very first time. He was trying to get home when he was met by the Devil! The Devil took him on a tour of Hell. He said he was screaming with pain all the way through the tour and he saw faces of familiar people and headless people bedecked with chains and other hellish things. When the devil was done with him he woke up in his bed screaming and his head was a splitting headache. He vowed that as long as he lived he would never take another drink. He spent the rest of his life telling about his trip to hell and to stop drinking the devils brew. The headache that Uncle Jake had was transferred to Aunt Jennie, strangely enough. She suffered for years with super headaches. She tried to alleviate them by grabbing the two children in her care, wards of the court. She threw them around and bounced them against the wall. She would wake them and make them scrub floors that had just been scrubbed. With this long-term torture trail she managed to make an idiot of the boy. A brother and sister acquired from the state, beautiful children were the brunt of her misery until she died.

Uncle Jake was a laugh, he had big floppy ears and over time when he turned his head they would flop, it was funny to see, but he was a good kind gentleman. Not many families have a Jake but it is a common name and I cherish that.

They lived in a cottage near the River Nith and in the spring there were daffodils, snowdrops, and crocus lining the road all the way down the main highway and were harvested and sold when they were near maturity and were very beautiful and commanded top monies.

The Threshing Machine

In the fall when the cold wind bites you its time for the thresher to come and they do. This giant machine can gobble up tons of oat straw and it takes about sixteen men and two boys to make it run efficiently, plus a stern boss. There was a thresher boss who takes care of the engine and the belts and the oiling. One man to the chaff, chaff is the outer coat of the oats. The chaff that drifts is the lightest and that is used for stuffing and put into bed mattresses and pillows and many different things and was a welcome thing, the threshing machine. The oats were separated inside the machine and came out their respective chutes into a burlap sack, which was hooked on at the end of the chute and depending on last year's crop they would be very busy and would have to move forward to the next stacks. There would be as many as 10 stacks in a row when they fired up this great engine it was marvelous to see, those great giant puffs of steam and the giant wheel start to turn and move the thresher, soon they were threshing again.

A big engine ran the thresher with a giant belt and sometimes this belt would break and everything would stop and every one took a rest but it wasn't long before the stern boss had everyone working and away they went. The giant drive wheel was driving the thresher, there were about sixteen men feeding the thresher and they had to be fed. There were more than likely about sixteen wives that prepared the food after the thresher shut down for lunch, and dinner.

Dinner was called noon lunch, lunch was not used then everyone headed for the kitchen and it was a sight to behold. The mountains of food and the happy faces of wives greeting all the farmers, with a quick hand wash. I don't remember if grace was said or not. I think the men were too nervous for that or it was not customary. They had lamb, pork, beef, potatoes, gravy, veggies, bread and some signal was given and the master picked up his fork and everyone dove in and the food disappeared before your very eyes, everything except some potatoes and gravy. Then came the pies and cakes, totally amazing food that was wolfed down and the pies and cakes. I was eating the blueberry pie and wondered if they might be our berries? Out came the pipes and cigarettes there were clouds of smoke and the doors of the liars club were opened, stories were told. The half-hour was soon gone and back to work they went all cigarettes and pipes, out! No smoking around or near the thresher, the places what were roped off, keep out! Or suffer the consequences.

When the stack got down near the bottom the mice started coming out, some stacks were infested. We had a job to kill these mice with the help of two dogs we did a good job. We took a break at three o'clock, fifteen minutes for tea, sandwiches, pastries; a smoke then back to threshing full bore. Carry on day after day until the threshing was done. Dinner was a carbon copy of lunch, abundance of food. All the farmers followed the thresher from farm to farm and that is how they got their manpower to run the beast! After the threshing was finished for a farmer the beast left and the next day the big clean up was on.

<<<<>>>>

Rocks and Rabbits

Bert, the neighbor boy and I went hunting rabbits one day, as we were walking along this tufted knoll Bert spotted a rabbit sunning him-self undercover. We made a wide swing around the rabbit without disturbing him; the three of us started making circles that we made smaller and smaller around the rabbit. Now this took some time but we kept moving slowly, slowly, round and round the rabbit. Then Jim threw a rock just when I dove on the rabbit. I was coming in from the left and Jim's rock came in from the right, the rock and I connected just above my right eyebrow! The scar is still there today. I was knocked silly for a while and the blood ran down my face. Bert said, "we had better go home." We never thought much about the blood. On the way home there was an occasional drop off my chin, but when we got home Mother saw me she thought I was killed, and went into a rage. She wanted to kill the neighbor boy but after she got me cleaned up it wasn't as bad as it looked and the rabbit? It got away.

<<<<>>>>

Maxwell Arms Hotel

When I got older I went into town to get a job, I got a job at a hotel as a bus boy, and the very first thing I did was go into the beautiful bathroom and sit on the seat. I sat there and felt so privileged but the flushing toilet was a strangely ingenious invention and mystery to me. I finally got up enough courage to push the lever down to flush and to stand and watch the water overflow. The water came from everywhere and I was sure it would overflow the bowl. Then suddenly it stopped boiling and quieted down, I flushed it over, and over again until I was sure everything worked all right, no flood. It felt good to be humanized, I earned a lot of tips and different kinds of people showed me how to make money. I also learned how to go up and down stairs with great speed. A bus boy to me is the most learned job of all. You have to read people and I did over and over for the next fifty years.

I missed my Mother, if things were not right I would talk it over with Mother. She always had a solution, she warned me of the people to watch out for, are the people who wear their smile upside down.

The hotel was hard work; I had to be up at 4:30 a.m. The first thing I did was to light the fires, one in the bosses room that was the control room. It was in the middle of everything. Then the dining room, that was a very large room and could seat many people. Next on the lighting of fires, "wrong" the kitchen was first, the heart beat of everything. I used to go very quietly to the kitchen and flip the light on; the cockroaches would scuttle at super speed everywhere. I would "back check" the fires to see if they were still burning. Most of the time they were, then I would light the fire in the social room; the milk testers stayed at the hotel and liked a cozy room. They came in 6:00 o'clock in the morning. After the fires were burning brightly I would pick up the shoes that were left outside the hotel room door to be polished and on more than one occasion would get the shoes mixed up. The hotel had about twenty bedrooms, I helped the maids with cleaning the rooms and making beds, and clean the bathrooms. Then those new words I learned were emphasized. The next was to clean the anti-rooms. These were little private party rooms, where you could have your special guests. The rooms had switches for numbered lights. Guests would push a button and a number would come up on a board in the hallway indicating which guest wished to use the room for parties. The rooms were a great moneymaker for the Maxwell Arms; it was hard work keeping them all up for the guests. I would take orders, carry trays, and bus the tables.

Then on to check the dining room to see how many had come for breakfast. One morning a couple came in they told me they were on their honeymoon and gave me their order. I gave it to the cook. Then I left to clean the anti-rooms and forgot all about the honeymooning couple in the dining room! I rushed in there with their cold breakfast and a thousand apologies and a humble stance. I could see they were more interested in gazing into each other's eyes and hadn't noticed I had forgotten them. When they left they even gave me a tip. I gave them one of my giant smiles and they left very happy. After breakfast cleanup we reset the dining room for lunch. I had to check the clock periodically all day then I would go to the butler's room, clean the silver and wash the "demitasse" cups. I always stuck my head in the kitchen doorway and said hello to the cook. That would get me something nice to eat, God help me if the fire went out. My vocabulary would increase immensely.

I started to get pains in my feet, which gradually got worse. I hoped and thought it would get better. I could fly up and down those stairs. There were three floors in all; my room was in the attic. I could count the boards on the roof. I finally couldn't walk I had to stay in bed with my feet elevated for days. That was one of the hardest things I ever did. I had to take big white pills every four hours, maybe calcium. I went to see the doctor and he told me my arches had collapsed. I had to get special shoes with arch supports and I would be all right. He told me I was on them too much, doing to much work and to slow down.

I had to leave The Arms and missed that place, all the different things I had to do, I surely learned a lot. I met every personality, like the one that had a penny coming in change and I didn't get it to him right away. He came looking for me and wanted to fight, but there were a lot of giant men there listening and he wouldn't dare start something, he soon backed down, so life goes on, ain't that so.

Tommy The Ferret

"Wee Tommy" our Ferret was a great little beast, he was a hard worker, if we could see signs of rabbits in the area we would wander around to look for the hopping trails of the rabbit. Rabbits come out mostly at night but like to come out and sun themselves during the day. Rabbits live in warrens below the ground. They like to dig their warrens on the sunny side of a hill. There are as many as twelve or more in a warren. This has to be analyzed because Tommy could get stuck down there and live off the rabbit meat for days! When the Ferret goes down into the warren, panic strikes through out the warren. You have to find all their exits and draw a string net over the hole and pound an anchor pin securely in the ground around each hole. Tommy knew, and got excited when a hunt was on. He jumped around in his box, waiting impatiently for all the holes to be netted. Then we took Tommy out; there is a certain way to hold him so he won't bite you. Hold him so he can't turn his head, then you put him down the hole. He saunters on down the tunnels, he saunters because Ferrets have a very strong smell and the smell terrifies the rabbits. About fifteen seconds later the ground started to rumble and out came the rabbits, they charged into the net at full force. We knocked their heads as fast as we could to kill them quickly (not for sport, this was dinner). Sometimes there is a scoot hole; this is an exit hole, only used in an emergency for such a time as this, very well hidden. Here they came one, two, three, full speed down hill and gone, two in the nets and the rest escaped. Then here comes Tommy sauntering out, we put him back in his box and he wants his prize, fresh rabbit liver. He was gentle if you held him just right!

Rabbit meat is very tasty, good meat, low in fat, no cholesterol, easy to skin, small in size, and could be eaten without aging. Tommy really knew his business, but once in a while he would den up, that is when the rabbit refuse to come out the hole and Tommy would eat on him for days. We could try to dig him out but it was better to put his box down there, leave your coat and come back later. Most of the time he was there waiting!

 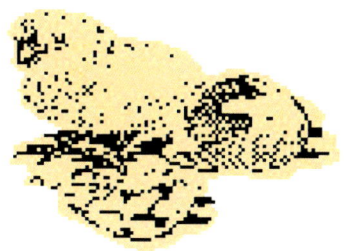

Ducks

Near the end of incubation of the chicken eggs something must have happened to the duck eggs or the hen. We switched the eggs from the hen and put them under the Mother Duck, in few days the little chicks started to hatch out and cheep around Mummy Duck. They were always hanging around the water and finally one-day she just swam out in the pond and they followed, and got all water logged and sank! All we heard was an occasional cheep. We thought it was peculiar at that time but it was the right thing for a Mother Duck to do she thought they were baby ducks and the chicks thought their mother was a chicken, much to our dismay.

Ducks are wonderful they keep your yard clean eating all the bugs, snails, they fertilize as they go along. They are wonderful to eat. You can use the down feathers for pillows and wing and neck feathers for typing fishing flies. You can become great pals. Ducks are smarter than chickens when they get dirty they go out in the water and take a bath. They don't have to be fed, they forage for themselves. Have you ever eaten a duck egg? They are delicious and you can only eat one, they are much larger than chicken eggs. It all adds up ducks are great.

WLA, School in England, Sheep, and Dody

We moved back and forth across the border between England and Scotland, following work, many times. When we lived in England I went to school in England, etc. I was in a fist fight every day. I was either winning or losing, how they hated the Scottish people and I learned to hate in return. I got to be pretty fast with my dooks; I lead off with my right or left. Mother and Margaret worked at the hostel, which was turned into a barracks and housed the Woman's Land Army (WLA). Mother was the Head Chef and Margaret was her helper. They made everything; they had a crew of WLA girls to do the work. Even I helped, just to be near the girls! They had a big truck to haul the girls around to work on the farms in the area. All the men had gone off to war the girls provided the (womanpower) to plant, cultivate, and harvest the fields producing food for the war effort. The girls ran the tractors and other field equipment; anything the farmers needed, the truck would pick them up again at night. It was a long day but our freedom was at stake and there were no other choices, everyone did their part.

While Mother cooked, Margaret and I had to go to school in the area. One of the girls at school was inattentive and had to sit in the front row so the teacher could watch her, she was doodling instead of doing her schoolwork. The teacher called her out in front of his desk and he took out his cane and bent her over the desk and gave her a brisk spanking. She threw a fit and started to scream, then he shook her. She kept on screaming he went and got this piece of Malaysian rubber and put her across his knee; he would whack her, she would scream, whack, scream, whack, scream, then finally she started to cry, and then sob. She was a different girl after that, she paid attention, and was a number one student, and she was moved to the back row.

Another day Margaret and I were on our way to school on our bicycle. We rode down this steep hill and had to round a sharp corner, we were going very fast, we made the corner all right, and right before us the road ahead was full of sheep!

\

Margaret was riding on the handlebars that made the bicycle hard to control. It was just like someone had taken a big knife and cut a slot through the herd of sheep. The sheep parted as if by magic, like Moses parting the Red Sea. We didn't touch a sheep! We left angry sheepherders with the surprise of their lives; they were yelling and shaking their fists at us for giving, them, the sheep, and us the scare of our lives.

Winter came and on that very same road we took the sled to school and we got going down that hill, we were laughing when we made that turn, Margaret was on the sled behind me and fell off. I didn't realize she was no longer on the sled. When I got to the bottom, no Margaret! I went back up the hill to pick her up and we had another good laugh. We weren't even late for school.

Dody

Near spring as time passed by, Dody had to go back to the Royal Air Force, and as he left to go North we accompanied him part way on that very same road. It was sad to see him go. Out there in the hills, there were no stone walls, no fences just sheep and us. We waved to him and it wasn't long before we couldn't see his arms waving any more. The sun was setting, it was mostly down hill and not much was said, on the way home, it was one of the more quiet times. As time went by it wasn't long before we heard pebbles on the windowpane, the familiar shout "Dody is Home," and the cycle began all over again. But it is never the same and those special moments of love, laughter, sorrow, farewells, joy, and greetings cannot be duplicated, just hold and savor them in your memory. Recall them when another set of circumstance prompts the beautiful memory and you will relive those special moments and emotions again and again. There are some special people in your life. Dody was one of them, may he rest in peace.

Salmon Run

The King Salmon are in and coming up the river, all sizes. Scotland held the record for weight and length for salmon for many a year and it was time for poachers to cash in. My Dad was one of them. He would catch those fish left and right and we would carry them home, they would be dragging on the ground. There was a bend in the river where the fish would backup and were easier to catch. We kept the fish in a wooden box and covered with a wet burlap sack. They didn't stay in the box long. They were soon sold, away they went into someone else's wooden box. All transactions were done at night but we had nothing to do with that-top secret. The black market was in full swing during the war years and everything was fair game. Whatever the market would bear, and salmon was at the top, the most in demand, the prize, very thinly sliced salmon, eaten raw with just a hint of smoke.

Gamekeeper and the Cook

My Dad would supply the big house with game, rabbits, pheasant, venison, and salmon. He would take orders from the cook and give them to the gamekeeper, who would get the game. One time the cook ordered a rabbit and complained the cat chewed on the rabbit. It was unsightly and not fit to serve to guests, so she took it home to feed her family. Please would he get another rabbit for the cook to serve to the Master's guests? No problem it was done, about a month went by and the same thing happened. Once again the house cat got the rabbit and chewed on it, she took it home to her family. Could he please get another rabbit for the guests? Oh no, my dad said, "this time you ate the cat" I hope it was good.

The gamekeeper would set a snare line and we would steal some of his rabbits on a regular basis, but I think he was wise to us, we needed rabbits too. The challenge goes on, to eat or not to eat. We carried game for the big shoot. Once a year in the fall flying birds ducks, grouse, and pheasants, were the prize and some we would hide and go back for them at night, for our family.

Pain of Frostbite

The cold winter days were upon us, we were into the minus numbers on the thermometer. We still had to go to school, we got the bikes out and away we went down the hill, I could feel the cold biting my hands, and ears. Finally we made it, but my hands and ears were frozen. I put my bike away and told the teacher in my classroom, my hands were cold. She said, for me to warm them by the fire! This was the wrong thing to do, when you have frozen hands and feet you must warm them up slowly. I did as she told me; needless to say that was the worst pain I ever endured in all my life. It was like being kicked by a cow, stung by a bee, or my worst beating ever, there is no pain like the pain I felt in my hands, and ears. Suddenly the teacher could see I was in great anguish and pulled me away from the fire. She put my hands in warm water in a classroom near by. The next day my hands and ears were severely swollen. Besides the pain, I was the object of much teasing and ridicule from kids in all classes. I remember well the most painful day in my life, so don't put your hands in the fire to get warm. Put them under your oxters (armpits) and warm them slowly.

Abandoned at The Train Station

I don't know how, I vaguely remember I went to the dog track races with Dad, or visiting some relatives. After the races were over at the track, Dad said, "just go the train station and get on the train and go to the Lazonby Station and then go home." I was eight or nine. I went to the train station but the train with the right name or number didn't come in or I didn't recognize it. I waited and waited. I had no money to buy anything to eat. All I could do was wait and wait. I watched intently, finally this man came along, probably the station agent, and asked me what I was waiting for. I gave him the whole story in five seconds flat. He told me he was the station "Detective" and said, "come with me." Then I started to cry and cry he checked me and said, "that will be enough of that." He took me to his office and told me to wait. He made a couple of phone calls and said I was going to stay with my Aunt in Carlisle, England. Who that was I didn't know, (she was a thin wholesome, buxom, beautiful woman). She was about thirty years of age, to me at my age that was about fifty. I had never seen her or heard of her before in my life. Then she called a taxi and it took me to her home, just like magic.

After I was at my Aunts house I told her the whole story about how I happened to be in this predicament. I was all worn out; they fed me and put me to bed, next to Grandpa's bed. This was late at night about two o'clock in the morning. The next day they took me to the train. When I got off the train and headed for home, Mother was waiting for me long before I got home. I knew she was stressed, she had a towel in her hands and was flailing that hand towel and crying, what happened to you? Again, I had to tell the whole story. She had imagined the worst, I was dead, abducted, stolen, or sold, my Rennie's home! I got the royal treatment. My Mother vented herself on Dad after he got home. It was awful to see how vicious a woman can be when she is defending her young, That's what it takes sometimes and she knew it. It took me a long time to get over that ordeal. I didn't like to go very far from home after that. I like to stay close to Mother; she was a good teacher! I was a willing student.

Winter

Only the living room and kitchen were heated during the winter. As the cold icy winds blew we slept in unheated bedrooms in the winter. There was no danger of fire. Mother gave us a little square of woolen blanket to warm our feet in bed. We held the blanket up in front of the fire by the stove until it was smoking and then we would make a mad dash for the bed. There was some fast moving when we thought they were just right. The blankets must have been warm enough, no one would get out of bed once you were snuggled down with that little blanket. Whenever the snow was blowing and the wind howling it was a time of appreciation to be all snuggled down in that bed. At night when the temperature dropped it could blow snow through any crack around the windows and pile it up on your bed. Mother would look in on us before she went to bed but it was more reassurance than any thing that all was well.

Keeping a path to the outhouse open had top priority in the winter and it was any ones or every ones job to keep the tank in the attic full of water via a hand pump, that was considered a kid's job.

John Campbell a cousin of my Mother and his new bride Anne came to our house for their honeymoon for two weeks. He was a nice young man. He worked in the coalmines; a blast had gone off a few years before in the mine and blew up in his face. We could still see the coal imbedded in is face. We would gaze at him in awe. He spent most of the time teaching Bert and me self-defense tactics and we just loved that. We had a great time together. We were taught the art of survival, which is a full time job.

We used peat moss for fuel to heat our home. They used a two-man spade to cut the peat moss for the fire. If the two men worked well together it was quite an art and fun to watch. The spade was razor sharp and they would dig in and then rock the spade making the job look easy! First you cut a ditch to drain the water off the peat; the peat moss was then stacked quite fancy. They were all thatched and have to remain stacked for two years to cure before they are used. The peat makes a nice warm fire, which can be banked and will hold all night, keeping your house nice and warm.

Life was tough but good and it seems we were busy all the time, carrying water, peat moss, and ashes in and out of the house. We didn't have time to play but were playing all the time. Our neighbor down the road had thirteen kids and they were busy, or to busy. They lived in a two- bedroom house! I sure wouldn't like the burden of all those children all day long, day in and day out, not quiet, and no peace. I sure hope they loved the Lord.

Saturday Night at The Dance

When it first started out there were only a few people that came and they would practice tuning up their instruments and do a few wiggles on the dance floor. Learning was the thing and that applied all the rest of my life. The music got better and word went out for a Saturday Night Dance that was exciting and it put a damper on everything when we couldn't stay up to watch the dancing. Eventually the Saturday night bash mushroomed into something swell and people came from everywhere and let their hair down. They didn't mind the small fee and people brought goodies galore. There must have been some kind of mind bender like beer, wine, or other booze but I was too young to know the difference. More and more people came to the dance on a Saturday night. The house was full of people and every room was full of activity. Then finally bang, boom the end, stop.

Someone said it was a bomb, an attack, but what it really was the floor had buckled under the load of all those people dancing! It only went down a few inches but due to all the stress from the war and everything of interest soon wound up !!at the Saturday Night Dance!!. Finally they peeled off in all directions and everything gradually got back to normal.

That Christmas my stocking was full of coal and ashes but I did get two oranges! I was grateful, the next year Margaret and I got a kaleidoscope. They all wanted to look a look at it and I said, "get away, no! You can't touch it." When I got tired of looking at it I finally relented and gave others a chance to see all the beautiful designs.

The blackouts came and things got serious, we had to check for light leaking through and around the curtains. We had to extinguish all lights before going outside. The closest bomb strike was about ten miles away. They called it a blockbuster and the vibration shook the dishes off the table. It was a relief for those days to end.

Three O'clock A.M.

Mother and Dody worked at the farm that was on the Army Base. They had to go through the base to get to their jobs. Mother and the rest of us thought we were on time. Usually they would be going past the guardhouse at 4 a.m. and somehow the alarm clock got messed up and it was two hours early. As they were going through this army base arm in arm going to work. As they passed the guardhouse, this booming voice called out, "who goes there, halt advance to be recognized, hands up, don't move." "Sargent of the Guard! enemy is the camp." Big lights came on and everything was upside down for a few minutes, once they found out they worked there, pointing up the road, at the farm. Then everything quieted down, the guards said we are in a state-of-war these guns are loaded and it is risky to walk through this camp like this. After apologies were offered all around they went about their way and said; we will be on time from now on, and we didn't mean to cause such a disturbance. They really thought it was 4:00 a.m. after all that commotion went on it was the correct time and time to go to work.

Brother George (Dody)

George, my oldest brother was as strong as a bull and was selected to join the Royal Air Force (RAF), and he did. He was gone for months, one night we heard something hitting the window, it happened again and again. Margaret got up to see what it was and she yelled loudly it was Dody! My brother, he is home! Instantly everyone was up and out of bed, down the stairs as fast as we could go to meet him and greet him. Home at Last! He was much wider it seemed and he was older looking for an instant I thought he was someone else but it was Dody all right.

He told us all about what he was doing and we all sat in a bunch as close as we could be for hours a healing thing to do, I would say. He never got into the war as it ended but he was ready. He was more serious after that, the war changed him or something changed him. We heard those little stones tapping on the window pane several time after that, and the greeting was always loud and clear. Even after he was out of the RAF we still heard those little stones on the window pane at night letting us know it was Dody, and he was home for a short visit, telling us of his adventures.

Jolly Farmers

I went to work for a different farmer, The Isles, was the name of the farm. The Farmer and his wife were big and jolly and loved the farming way of life. He and his wife were a good team. I was skinny and there was a conspiracy to change me into one of them! Porridge for breakfast with cream, bacon, eggs, (four eggs for me) stacks of toast, "home grown bacon and eggs," jelly or jam for the toast. They both ate alike worked alike, they almost dressed alike. I went out to the field to put up stooks that had been cut and bound with the binding machine the day before and left overnight. I worked for a couple of hours and here they come with a big basket of sandwiches and a kettle of tea and a cloth napkin, white no less and helped me finish up.

We went back to the farm to the Granary; the farmers in the Shire (like a county) would bring their bags of grain to be processed from the thresher. The grain was in 100-pound sacks. My job was to take the sacks to the machines in the Granary for the grain to be cleaned rolled, etc. I think they were giving me a test of strength. The sacks were on trucks and it was easy to flip them onto my back, the hard part was getting up the thirteen steps to the granary. I flipped the sack high on my shoulder and adjusted it in order to carry this big load and away I went, never looking back. I almost lost it on the twelfth step but regained my balance and finished my test! They were saying I would never make it, that skinny lad.

After I came down from the loft they took me to the cow barn and introduced me to the cows, beautiful Jerseys and all hand milked. They were big and fat like the farmers. There was a continual rapport between the farmer and his wife just bordering on insult.

Sunday was the next day and they asked me if I would like to go church, I said I would, they told me the time to be ready, I was there and away we went. He was still grumbling about something, and he was sort of not driving a straight line, she complained and he gave the steering wheel a good upward jerk and handed it to her and asked her if she would like to drive! The car veered off the road and ended up in the ditch and he landed on top of her, she was screaming for him to get off and I learned a whole new vocabulary in five minutes. After self esteem was restored we were dropped off back to the farm by a tractor. My Dad had worked on that farm when he was a young lad.

Holiday in Glasgow

Holidays, I hate holidays, I didn't ever want to be away from Mother. Glasgow, I hated it there. Your Uncle Jim Shields is there and he is my brother, he is a nice man. Uncle Jim and Aunt Jean lived in a tenement apartment house. It was old and rundown. There were bugs in the walls, bugs everywhere they would bit you. Mother's mother Grandma Shields lived there also. Uncle Jim said we are going meet her. Well we did, she chewed tobacco and smoked cigarettes and spit in this spittoon across the floor. She never missed as if each shot was a challenge. Breakfast was a challenge, porridge with sour skim milk. Some kind of sour pancakes for lunch and my treat was fish and chips at night. I couldn't eat much away from Mother. She told me to keep healthy. The best thing I liked was going to the animal shelter and see all those dogs and cats. It was such a long walk there and back. I liked to look at all the stuff in the shop windows, my introduction to window-shopping.

Poverty was everywhere, there were no fat people, just eat what you could get. Briton was at a low ebb, down and almost out. There was a bombed out place where you could still get into the cellar and I got to know the kids around the neighborhood. We would play "post office." I don't remember what it was but there sure was a lot of kissing and change partners and more kissing. The bonny ones got the most kissing.

The holiday was soon over and home again, I had lost weight. I don't know if it was all that kissing or the bad food that caused the weight loss. Poor people they did their best and were sorry to see me go I couldn't go fast enough to get home. I got the royal welcome from my family. I ate and slept for days and then I was all right. I was soon back in school trying to learn something and the schoolmaster was trying to put it there. The learning part, Mr. Pace my school master a hard man to forget, I used many of his examples during my lifetime.

The Lions

We lived at estate called "The Lions." Across the valley there was an estate called "The Fox's" and nair the twain shall meet. The Foxes seemed to be nice people. My Dad was the gardener and he also took care of the game, like wild game pheasant, ducks, rabbits, and salmon. We had a cage to age the game, made out of 1/8" mesh wire to keep the blow flies out and when the meat turned blue it was ready to eat. The cook made some spectacular dishes for the gentry. My dad got a ham once, the cook said my dad could have it, it was full of maggots. My dad took it home and put it in boiling water and they came wiggling out in a hurry. He threw in a handful of salt and that got rid of the smell. The ham disappeared or it was changed into something else.

Out cat had a litter of kittens on Dad's bed and everything got wet Dad came home picked up the cat and kittens and threw them out in the snow. They were dead in a few minutes. That made us all very unhappy. To retaliate for such action, I went to the shed and got a can of roofing nails and put them point up one by one all the way across the road. It was a fierce array, my attacking army, invincible! Occasionally I heard thunder off in the distance but it didn't look much like rain, I was waiting for a car to come along and watch the tires go flat. I heard that rumble again, but it was not a car, not thunder, but they were army tanks. Great big tanks, one tank after the other, a whole army rolling down the road over my tacks. After the tanks were past I looked and nearly all the tacks were gone. What a good laugh I got out of that, all joined in, the joke was on me. The tanks disappeared for parts unknown and the rumble slowly dissipated. My Uncle Willie came to visit and brought his dulcimer and all the neighbors came to hear him play. We had a party with dancing and all the fixings; we had a great time. It brought a lot of people together that were standoffish or reserved. They became good friends before we parted. There were cakes, pies, scones, packed for them to take to help them on their way; this was the parting tradition when you had a social gathering.

Foxes and Chickens

Some one didn't take their walk one night to check that everything was secure and the animals were safely tucked away. They didn't close the chicken house door, when morning came there were feathers as far as you could see and an endless trail of feathers leading away from the chicken house.

The farmer said, we could follow the trail and try to find the Fox's lair. Two of us started on the trail it was easy to follow. We kept on for hours and hours, drumming up a good appetite was about all we did. It was noon and the trail started to get smaller and by 3:00 o'clock in the afternoon it was hard to find feathers to keep going and finally we just gave up. The foxes had us pegged; they had out foxed us. I am sure they were just ahead in that scraggy hillside watching us with their kit pups to feed. I realized it was that time of year and they were enjoying the bounty. So lock your chickens in their house at night, Mr. Fox is watching you and calculating his next move on your unguarded stock. Mr. Fox is always wearing a smile and keeps his teeth clean at your expense.

The Bus

Mother said I had to go to Dumfries for something but I can't remember what it was, she gave me the money for bus fare and away I went. It was up hill to the bus stop and I started to get anxious about the bus coming. I decided to climb that big pine tree that would give me a look way down the road. So up the tree I went, higher and higher, it was so exciting. If I could only make it one more branch up then I would be able to see way down the road for the bus. Then the unthinkable happened! The branch broke and down I came, getting slapped by branches on the way down. I was suddenly stopped by a barbed wire fence that broke my fall and cut deeply into my leg, just below my right knee. The pain was like that of a dog bite and the blood was suddenly there and running down my leg and into my shoe. Then, here comes the bus, I ran to it and got on. The bus driver yelled at me for getting blood all over "his" bus. He wanted me to get off! But the old ladies on the bus had compassion for me and tried to help. Some people were indifferent; most people wanted to know what happened, as if it would make any difference.

Anyway I got to town and did my errand, and started on my way home with dozens of different reactions from people, however, the one I didn't expect was a verbal tongue lashing and some rough handling for being so stupid and that I had ruined my "shoes!" After Mother's towel ringing and stress everything quieted down but Mother sill had empathetic groanings for me as if she had all the pain, and was ever so gentle as she bandaged my wound with diligence.

If I could only remember just what I had to get at the store and the need for the bus ride it would be all o.k. and would have been worth it. Maybe it was mundane but I don't know for sure, some things in life you never know, or you don't need to know, are deemed to be and will be.

Swans

Mother sent me to the Vennel Bakery to purchase three loaves of bread, The Vennel was where all the buses came together and you could get on a bus and go anywhere in the Shire District. I was waiting for my bus and I had a lot of time to spend so I decided to go and sit on the wall by the river that gently flowed out to the sea, and was great for fishing. As I was sitting these I saw these two mute swans. They were swimming toward me making this ca, ca, ca noise as if they wanted something, I realized they must be hungry! Well the bread I purchased at the bakery was exposed, I was fondling the strips of bread and tore off a piece of bread and threw it to the swans, well they said, "thank you", with louder ca, ca, ca's in order for me to hear them. They begged for more, more ca, ca, ca's -- more bread. I told them to stop doing that; the bread had to go home, for our family. I kept picking off little pieces and soon I had a big hole in the bread. I told the swans no more bread, but they kept ca, ca, ca'ing it was great entertainment, and also as I was feeding the swans I looked at the loaf and it was almost gone! That is when I realized I was in trouble. The loaf of bread was gone, Mother would kill me, Dad would kill me, I am dead. How could I get out this one? Well I realized I could not get out of this one! Just face the music, and I did. Just don't let a swan talk you out of a loaf of bread with a few ca, ca's. After I explained what I did and dusted off my pants, Mother asked me how I liked my soup without bread. This one time I was mute! Some things are better unsaid than left to provocation. Whenever I go to town, I look over to the river wall to see if the swans are there and make sure I haven't any bread with me that they can ca, ca, me out of.

 # The Mouse

It gets dark early in the winter, the cold wind makes you huddle a little closer to the fire or add another piece of coal. The kitchen fire was always the last one to go out. If you sit still and keep still you could hear him come running on the linoleum floor. The mouse was making his rounds; he would run along the wall and stop at the doorway, wait a few seconds then cross the doorway and run across the hearth. Checking for food scraps, we left him some cheese once in a while which he took back to his home on a dead run following his trail. There are not many places left where you can hear a mouse run on the floor! We had to check on the mouse population and not get too many; they can be destructive if left unchecked.

We had one of Grandpa's old pipes with a broken stem. We would squeeze a piece of cheese into the pipe and turn a bowl upside down and prop it with the pipe. The bowl of the pipe and the cheese must be facing in! It won't be long before you hear the clunk of the bowl coming down over the mouse. Then you had to lift the bowl up quickly and flatten the mouse with your other hand, that way he has some chance to escape. This is not a job for the squeamish; beginners can wear a glove! But what good is a house without a mouse. You must leave some for the cats, if you have mice you won't have rats, if your nose is in tune, you can smell the mice. You can't surprise mice very often like when he is sitting in your parlor having his dinner, if you don't move he will climb up your leg and then you can flatten him! Yuk.

The Kiss

Kisses come in all sizes, and all flavors, there are tender kisses, mushy kisses, good by kisses, hello kisses, a kiss that has a snap in it. The silent one, and the worthless kiss. You can have the most beautiful girl in the world and if she has a dead kiss it means nothing. Marriages are built on one kiss. Time away makes the kiss grow stronger, the age and the sex makes a kiss what it is. Whatever age a woman is that's how long she has been practicing how to kiss. The woman is the responder and if she does that right it will be right. But my first kiss, a girl walked up to me, put her arms around me and laid a big kiss on me. No words were spoken, first eye contact then lip contact. Truly a great experience. We parted and never saw each other again, and strangely enough I don't know what she looked like. She stole my first kiss and I will never get it back. If I could, I would give it to Elsie.

Poverty Bowl

Food was getting scarce in Briton during the war and us kids in school got a supplemental soup line. We had to be on time or no soup. People that made this soup it was like in a home. Anyone could have made the soup and got their government check. But this soup was like the worst most pitiful soup I ever came across. They gave us a bowl, round and white and about 4 inches across and to this day I still call it a poverty bowl because that's what was in it, pure poverty. Dirty dishwater with a few fat globules floating around and 1 piece of onion and hard bread. It took a cook and three adults to supervise the doling out of this deplorable mess they called soup. Somehow we struggled through and survived the war and I think often of the poverty bowl that stays in our cupboard and gets to come and be filled with hearty wholesome soup. Which I enjoy to the fullest!

 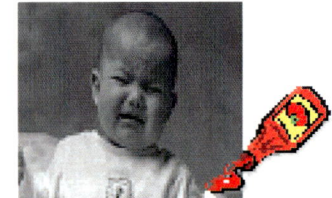 

Dody and The Catsup

My Mother told me the story of my oldest brother Dody when he was little between two and three years old, he was sound asleep in his crib and my Dad said to my Mother, "let's go to the movies". Mother said, "Oh no! We have no one to watch Dody." Dad said, "he will be all right, he has just eaten, he is dry, and asleep for the night." After much coaxing Mother conceded, they hopped on their bikes a former way of transportation to the movies. Well, Mother didn't say what the movie was about; all she did was worry about Dody. Finally after much convincing that they should go home, she had a feeling that everything was not well at home, so away went and in great haste rushed home. They hurried into the house and sure enough, there was Dody all covered with blood and not moving. Mother went into hysterics and was screaming which brought the neighbors, they were aghast! Some one had murdered her little boy, what oh what, have they done to that poor boy. With all the noise going on, Dody woke up, stood up and smiled, Dad said it's only catsup!

The fright of Mother's life turned out to have a happy, funny ending. Needless to say no one could ever talk her into leaving her babies at home asleep again while she went to the movies. Mother was the best Mother in the world. She raised all her children to adulthood. A rare thing in those days with childhood illness, no vaccines, and not too much in the way of pediatric care. Mother was the greatest!

The Letter G

It was in the fall when we went back to school and went through the pecking order. We had a writing test and we came to the letter g and I unintentionally went below the line like instead of g on the line. She slammed me on the back of the head several times and got me into a nervous state, which caused me to write the letter g below the line again. Well something clicked in my head and I wrote the letter way down the page covering several lines. When the teacher saw that, something clicked in her head and she went into a rage. She shook me like a rag doll, she yelled, I yelled, and the head master came in and dismissed the class. Nothing else was ever said about the letter g below the line, a case of classical reverse psychology!

47

Sister Margaret and Brother Dody

My sister Margaret has high energy, adaptable to anything, a most likeable person, type A personality, and could turn her hand to anything. Most of all she wanted to dance. When Saturday night came there would always be a dance somewhere and surely you would find Margaret and Dody there kicking up their heels. Dody like dancing almost as much as Margaret did, they would practice new steps in the cow barn while doing the milking. They turned the radio up and danced between the rows of cows to be ready for the next Saturday night dance.

Dody liked one other thing more than dancing and that was reading. He wanted to read all the time, anything he could lay his hands on. He led a secretive life apart from the Dody we knew. We really didn't know too much about him just the parts he wanted you to know. He was four years older than I was and that would account for some of that. He consistently had a new and beautiful girl on his arm. They always looked so happy; but he ended up marrying a schoolteacher, and newspaper editor. They had no children, but were well matched and lived a happy comfortable life.

Chocolates

During the war food was scarce as hens teeth but there always seemed to be enough to go around. I had this craving for chocolates with soft centers, for there were none around and this was only a dream. The war moved on and so did time, we heard the news that chocolate was going to be available again and plenty of it. I checked every day at the store but no chocolate appeared. It seemed I would go crazy for want of chocolate. Then one day on my way to the store I heard that chocolate had arrived in town. I couldn't get to the store fast enough and promptly got in line for two boxes of chocolates with soft centers. I was like a miser guarding his gold; I opened the box with care and diligently popped one in my mouth and savored the sweetness of that candy and the aroma of the chocolate and chewed it and popped in one after the other with great speed. I was on box two before you could blink twice, by the middle of the second box I started to slow down and savor the soft centers. By the end of the second box I just couldn't eat the last one, my craving was over, finished, done! I could eat no more. Then this feeling came over me, a strange weakness, then a careless feeling, the moments flew by and a great pressure built up in my stomach, then it broke loose. My whole glutinous escapade with chocolates came to an inglorious end. I was the sickest guy in town and I wished I could die and I did.

Margaret and The Oil Stove

It was a busy day as usual around the house and everyone had his or her jobs to do. We had this three in a row burner stove, oil fired, Mother asked Margaret to light the stove, they were going to make bread or cook something big, Margaret said, "o.k. and ran off to light the stove. Now it's no easy chore to light the stove, it has to be primed and preheated. You just don't rush the job, if you rush the stove you can get to much oil in the feed trough for the other burners. Then overflows and drips into the catch pan, which it did. The flame followed the oil, Mother Called to Margaret to see if everything was all right. No answer, Mother called again and no answer, then Mother went to see what was wrong and there stood Margaret with the stove on fire! Margaret stood there transfixed in an angelic stance with her arms folded across her chest, in shock, her head in submission looking down at the floor. She kept telling Mother she didn't mean it, and she was sorry. Mother did a little dance of frustration and finally wrapped her towel around the burning burner and the fire was snuffed out in a jiffy. We had a substantial amount of smoke but not enough to bring in the fire brigade.

Everything eventually settled down and got back to normal, Margaret and Cathie's doll came back from the doll doctor, a window was put in the outhouse, we all learned to ride bikes; however, just one last lesson on how to ride a bike. We (Bert and I) took Margaret up a hill to teach her to ride a bike. We gave her a big push, she couldn't make the turn at the bottom of the hill, and she hit the stone wall and flipped over into the stinging nettle bushes and came out screaming. That was the first time my sister swore at me, it was a real bad word, you bugger! She called me a bugger. We both pushed you. Your both buggers, she yelled! It must have really been painful. We carried the bike home!

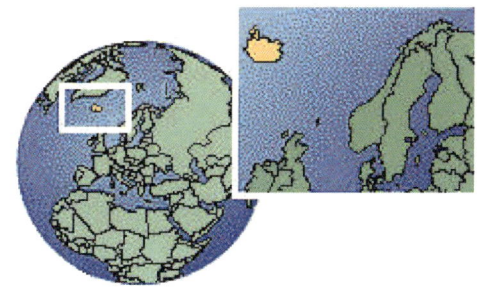

To America

It was a long way through the hills and through the little towns one after the other. I was on my way to America. I was excited as I got on the bus it seemed the bus was travelling so slowly. The destination was Ayre. A small air port comparison wise to airports in large cities. Everything was so strange to me; even the people were nice and polite. I had hardly been in a car let alone an airplane that was a double-decker and had a piano room, a bar, and circular stairway! My brain was working overtime loading in all the modern technology. We were buckled in then up and away we went with propellers and four engines roaring. The pilot was in communication with the ground and control tower when we finally got the all clear, then we were really on our way to America (no!) We had to go to Rikavik? Iceland for breakfast. We had pancakes, syrup, sausage, and ham, anything you wanted. What were pancakes? It was great to see all that ice and snow over that country when we took off this time. The Captain invited me up to the cabin cockpit and I gladly accepted the invitation. I was amazed at what I saw, huge

banks of rolling clouds as far as I could see; all shapes and you could fly right through them. He pulled the stick back and moved the plane higher and we were above the big beautiful clouds as far as we could see, infinite, and endless. I think the airline was Pan American. I was free to roam all over the plane and I did and they were after me with questions and I them. I think they wanted to hear my Scottish brogue.

By the time we landed in Boston, I was a full-fledged pilot and by lingual in any tongue. Are we in America? We are in America was the answer, Boston, Massachusetts. I had to get my luggage and go through customs. All that waiting and look at all those black people, zillions. I'd never seen black people in Scotland, just read about them in Little Black Sambo in school. The first car I saw was a Chevrolet.

Then it was through customs. The customs agent said, "open your suitcase." It's only my working clothes, "sir." I replied, "open your suitcase son." I did and the smell just about knocked him over! What is that smell? He slammed the suitcase shut. Again, "what smell, Sir." By now the suitcase was closed. I had brought my work clothes from the cow barns, I didn't think they would smell bad. My hobnailed boots were covered with fresh cow manure. What a great aroma permeating the area and I was getting not so happy looks. He opened this bag and looked in and pulled out my two sandwiches, packed by the lady I worked for on the farm. He threw them in a box and told me to move on, "next he cried." By this time my eyes were watering, what do I do now? My lunch gone! "Exit." I knew what that meant, by now, so exit I did.

I hadn't gone very far when there he was, my brother Dody, Mom, Bert, and Cathie. I hardly recognized him; he was so mature looking. Everyone let me do the talking, just listening to my accent, was like pie from home. Big squeezes, big hugs, big smiles and big steps out of that Boston airport. We are in America! Eye! On the way home we stopped at Howard Johnson's and had banana splits in this America, or heaven, the skinny kid was home. **God Bless America!**

"Na greeten."

Thanks Elsie my little one, Ren!

The Family all settled in the United States in Jaffrey, New Hampshire

Front Row – George (Dody), Mother Saville, Cathy

Back Row – Rennie, Margaret and Bert

Circa - 1960

About the Author

Rennie lives the successful Christian life with Gods' word as his guide; he carries boundless enthusiasm, enduring love for his large family, toward all of God's creatures, and most of all to God this present day.

A strong, yet gentle man, as described in the story "The Kiss," this book is a special gift as we celebrate our twenty-third wedding anniversary on Valentine's Day!.